CONT

MW01286019

FOREWORD

MR. REALISTIC III

KEEPING IT REAL III

SUPPORT YOUR OWN

THE REEL TEAM

THE REEL TEAM II

THE REEL TEAM III

CREATOR'S WORDS

CREATOR'S WORDS II

THE CHURCH

THE CHURCH II

THE CHURCH III

DEAR JOU'VERT

COLORED RELATIONSHIP

I GOT

SUPERSTARS

SUPREME LOVE

SUPREME LOVE II

SUPREME LOVE III

PERFECT LOVE

PERFECT LOVE II

FOR PARENTS ONLY

FOR PARENTS ONLY II

FOR PARENTS ONLY III

FOR PARENTS ONLY IV

FOR PARENTS ONLY V

FOR PARENTS ONLY VI

FORWARD

Allow me to introduce myself. I, Mr. Dave R. Queeley also known as Mr. Realistic or John de Baptizer was born on St. Thomas on July 5 to the late Walsort R. "John" Queeley and Barbara B. Thomas. I am a 1988 graduate of the Ivanna Eudora Kean High School, Home of the Devil Rays.

I created Reel to Reel Production, an upcoming company dedicated to giving the youth of this community a voice through the written medium. I am no stranger to some of the issues that has been plaguing our communities and neighborhoods, so it is in my view to favor or sponsor ideas that make sense, challenging our communities and neighborhoods and all young people to re-think the customary ways of doing the Creator's works and carrying out the original plan which is, "GOOD WILL CONQUER EVIL AND LOVE WILL TRIUMPH OVER HATE."

I have now made myself the new voice of example to all Mahogany males. In the 21st century we are now living like we are bullet proof and that crime does pay. We need to channel our anger into positive change in our lives and to teach our youth that their feelings, attitudes and actions have serious consequences. My writings are informative and inspiring to turn as many hearts, souls, and lives to returning to having respect, love, and good intentions for one another on a daily basis.

This is something Joe Bogus aka the government system or police department cannot do; help me lift the spirit and give hope. Today we are going to lift spirits and give hope to all. One thing I've learned is no matter what I'm writing it's always suppose to move the masses to do what's right and to be positive in life. My writings are lightening rods from the Creator so that non truth seekers aka evil doers may wake up and receive their mental and spiritual blessing that leads to prosperity and being successful in life.

Once again, THANK YOU for buying and reading this book.

THE TRUTH IS FREEDOM!

Mr. Dave R. Queeley
CEO/Founder of Reel to Reel Production

MR. REALISTIC III
The Reform Hooligan
By
Mr. Dave R. Queeley

KABOOM!! Guess who's back, it's the reformed hooligan. Don't shoot the messenger, just listen to the message. Mr. Realistic is only just another vehicle from Creation to spread the Good News that the Creator is Love and not hate. Mr. Realistic will only be a reporter of the Good News that the Creator's original plan will be fulfilled in the future like prophecy. GOOD WILL TRIUMPH OVER EVIL AND LOVE WILL TRIUMPH OVER HATE.

Young people must be open minded about listening to what Creation has to offer because it will help change their life and mind. If they read what Creation has written they are really going to get enlightened about the battle of Good over Evil. Mr. Realistic wants to be known as someone who put something great on this earth. His ultimate goal in life is just to have timeless and classic writings that will help save young people and children from the cesspool of madness that is life. They can't stop searching and fighting for the truth to be told and heard. They have been risking their life for a very long time serving and working for Satan and his Angels of Destruction.

Mr. Realistic wants all people, young and old, to know these words are the manifestation of reality and truth. Mr. Realistic is a living testimony that crime does not pay. He also is someone who continues to take his life in the right direction so that young people can see it's never too late to change or join the battle of good over evil. Especially when they have grown up in a crime infested area.

Mr. Realistic is here to tell them they can change their lives if they want too because he shares their frustration. He is one of those people who has little or no money but have a lot of heart, strength and fight to continue the battle of good always over evil. I am not a politician or government official but a true worker for mental, economical and spiritual change and freedom of young people and children who now have no vision or morals. They see having respect, love, and good intentions as some sort of bad disease.

Young people need someone real to lead them through the present swamp of doom they have been living with for decades. Mr. Realistic will support anyone who will take a stance and share their outrage at the fact that young people now have no real representation in our government system. The ones who start out looking out for the children and young people eventually sell out to the pressures of doing what's wrong because it's big business. It makes more money than doing what's right. Mr. Realistic is asking all people (black or white) to make the very large leap of faith and return to love, respect and good intentions and the Creator's original plan of GOOD WILL TRIUMPH OVER EVIL AND LOEVE WILL TRIUMPH OVER HATE.

The deterioration of having respect, love, justice and good intentions did not happen overnight, it took years; so it will take years to rebuild it. Mr. Realistic is tired of love, respect and good intentions diminishing status in our communities and neighborhoods. If gun violence and crime continues to happen with all these random, senseless and unnecessary homicides and assaults that continue to happen every other day, week and month. Gun violence and crime is very much alive and it's killing our young people and children. They need to be taught how to become living revolutionaries for love, respect and good intentions.

Mr. Realistic and the Common Sense Movement are always on the front lines of the battle of Good over Evil fighting to see that children and young people are no longer in mortal danger at their schools, on the streets, and at the mall. Mr. Realistic will help the undecided make up their minds, whether they want to join the Common Sense Movement and continue the battle of Good over Evil.

When Mr. Realistic starts shining, he will be shining as bright as a star. Society will have no other choice but to notice it. His words and writings are words of a reformed hooligan who was sent by

Creation to tell the people wake up and live. Mr. Realistic the new
PHENOMENAL MAN.

READ THIS AND WEEP, HATERS. KABOOM!!
I'M OUT!

KEEPING IT REAL III
By
Mr. Dave R. Queeley

REAL VERSUS COUNTERFEIT

Samuel Blyden, back at you once again. Checking the brothers to see if they learned anything from the first two. So if they did not, it's time to duck down because here comes the Truth again.

Keeping It Real or being real has now become completely devoid of its meaning of Truth. It keeps on being infiltrated by counterfeiters who don't care about the rules or laws of life and the Creator's original plan which is, "GOOD WILL CONQUER EVIL AND LOVE WILL TRIUMPH OVER HATE." Returning to having respect, love, justice and good intentions will be an important and encouraging step forward in disrupting Satan and his Angels of Destruction's counterfeit Lacosa Nostra's organization that continues to bind foolish young people to a life of crime and violence.

Young people must deal in reality; and the reality is that gun violence, drugs and crime are taking their lives faster that they can graduate from high school or college. The vow of KEEPING IT REAL or SILENCE IS THE KEY that was once part of the oath to Lacosa Nostra's is more myth than reality in the 21st century because now gangsters are willing to wear wires and to testify for the prosecution against another gangster in exchange for leniency in their own cases. That's why the street justice continues to be "kill or be killed".

Some young people think going to jail or prison will make them hard core or obtain a higher rank in their gang. That's why they continue to drink the poisoned Kool-aid of injustice that continues to make sure there will be blood and body organs spilled on the street. They have forgotten prison is not a luxurious place and the education received there will not serve the inmate well once he/she returns home to the free world. Young people must understand that prison is nothing more than a modern day concentration camp and slavery at its best.

Glorifying the ghetto, gun and gangster culture is now the modus operandi for Keeping It Real in the 21st century, and the reality is that there is no glory or value in living in the cesspool of doom (prison or jail) or on the front lines of death. Keeping It Real is suppose to be about having a positive impact, not a negative impact on the communities and neighborhoods we live in.

A negative impact is SAGGIN, which means NIGGAS backwards. The sagging pants trend started in prison, where it was the calling card to let other prisoners know you were a homosexual. In the 21st century some so called gangsters are still continuing this practice as a fashion statement in our schools, malls, communities and neighborhoods. This trend has grown immensely popular in both white and black males and they must be taught emulating prisoners or any other group without understanding what they stand for is dangerous.

A positive impact will be to return to having respect, love, justice and good intentions for one another like back in the good old days of understanding and unity. All the senseless, random and unnecessary killings and shootings are undeniable proof that gun violence, drugs and crime are out of control and there is now no understanding or unity in our communities and neighborhoods.

There is an old saying to describe what's now happening in the 21st century and its "United we stand and Divided we fall." Gun violence, drugs, and crime has destroyed what little togetherness or Keeping It Real we had as a people who were once seekers of justice and non violence. They knew the Truth was stronger than any drug or violent act. In the 21st century everyone must play their part in lowering the fatality rate because gun violence, drugs and crime continue to escalate out of control.

Keeping It Real wants all young people to ask themselves this one question, "Who is bringing in the illegal weapons, ammunitions by the carts or the drugs by the tons?" The answer will be the same, it's not the street man; it's the people in high places with money and power. Keeping It Real or being real is nothing more than a cliché because young people ultimately do what is convenient and in their own best interest. Sometimes that means turning a Confidential Informant (CI), which means SNITCHING.

Keeping It Real is now a "wolf in sheep's clothing" and it's like telling your lover, "Baby I love you. That's why I think this separation will strengthen our relationship." NO, it won't strengthen the relationship; it means the relationship is over. It isn't real anymore, it's counterfeit.

Keeping It Real now has no fiscal reality. It's like Hollywood, full of fakers. Keeping It Real is always allergic to haters and counterfeiters because haters and counterfeiters are always faking it until they make it; never KEEPING IT REAL. They are always running away from the TRUTH.

KEEPING IT REAL PART III

SUPPORT YOUR OWN
United by Artistic Ambition
By
Mr. Dave R. Queeley

Stop putting strangers on a pedestal or before your own kind. It's time to start supporting all local artists before they are famous or on TV. Local people don't want to spend their money to see local artists practice their talents, but will spend hundreds of dollars to see a stranger practice his/her talent, get paid and take the bag of money back to their homeland to big up their home economy. It's time We the People start supporting all local artists as one of the new exports that is coming out of our communities and neighborhoods on a daily basis; instead of only the bad news of Black on Black Crime.

Supporting local artists can be a real true solution to our financial problems and situations in the future. Music, art and word power are three things that can bring people and world together. So let's get on the band wagon before it's too late. We the People have to remember before these strangers became superstars, they were local artists in their home land and their communities and neighborhoods supported them until they hit it big time. That's the same thing our communities and neighborhoods have to do before our local artists make it big time. Like the old time saying, "A good man or woman is never honored in their home town."

The time has come to change this evil and negative mentality of self destruction and death because it really takes a village to raise a positive child. It's time to free up the respect, love and good intentions for all local artists. Supporting local artists will bring unprecedented financial growth to our communities and neighborhoods that are so desperately needed to stop all those senseless, random, and unnecessary shootings and killings that continue to be negative examples of Good over Evil.

In the 21st century no one working for Joe Bogus aka the Government is the major spokesperson for supporting local artist's aspirations, but some of them are always ready and willing to support strangers with thousands of dollars instead of supporting their own. We the People have to start supporting local artistic beauty like it's a rare Michael Angelo painting up for sale.

SUPPORT YOUR OWN NOW.

THE REEL TEAM
By
Mr. Dave R. Queeley

The Reel Team is the New Renaissance in the 21st century.

The Reel Team is firing off a head shot to all professional athletes, movie stars, rappers, r&b singers or whatever your occupation is, who were born in the Virgin Islands and made millions of dollars and got rich and switch from the love, respect and good intentions that helped them when they were kids growing up in the VI.

The Reel Team will be the new sheriff of respect, love and good intentions in our communities and neighborhoods and they are calling out to all the members of THE VI RUNAWAY LOVE CLUB to do better. It's time for all professionals to stop investing where they live and start investing where they were born. It seems to the Reel Team that they have forgotten "what came in the beginning will come in the end". They were born in the VI and some of them will be buried in the VI. Instead of staying away complaining about how bad or hard things are in VI, they can come back home and join the Reel Team of GOOD CONQUERING EVIL AND LOVE TRIUMPHING OVER HATE, and help find true solutions to all the killings and shootings.

Truth seekers would think people who were born in the VI and made millions of dollars there would be 24 hr community centers on all three islands for our young people to have something to do in a supervised environment while their parents are at work, sometimes two and three jobs just to make ends meet. There are no excuses because money can move a mountain in the 21st century.

These professionals are acting like they have amnesia because they are forgetting how hard it is growing up in the VI with nothing to do. With their star powers they can help solve some of the major problems of the people of the VI, like all the unsolved murders and shootings. They can become elected government officials or law enforcement officers because they already have financial freedom so Satan's angels of Destruction will find it hard to bribe them into serving injustice and darkness aka planned doom.

The Reel Team will focus attentions on the deteriorating situation of respect, love and good intentions and the growing presence of evil, sinful ways and disrespect in our communities and neighborhoods. The Reel Team will not be a quick fix process; it will help our communities and neighborhoods to experience a new freedom of respect, love and good intentions in the midst of all the difficulties while trying to fight off Satan's angels of destruction, who continue to poison their lives.

The Reel Team will take respect, love and good intentions from out of the back room of hate and to the forefront of our communities and neighborhoods and to help usher in the awareness and information about how important it is for GOOD TO CONQUER EVIL AND LOVE TO TRIUMPH OVER HATE. The Reel Team will help youths to see something positive happening in their communities and neighborhoods and they will want to join the team to make their communities and neighborhoods a better place to live or visit without hearing automatic gun fire at night time.

The Reel Team will put the genie of injustice and darkness aka planned doom back in the bottle and to help achieve the greatest UNITY our communities and neighborhoods have ever seen.

THE REEL TEAM-KEEPING IT REAL!

THE REEL TEAM II
THE DISRESPECT STOPPERS
By
Mr. Dave R. Queeley

CRIME DOES NOT PAY

Do the crime you do the time, there will be no more slaps on the wrist or pat on the back for anyone charged with possession of an unlicensed firearm during the commission of a crime of violence. It's time our court system stop giving out bail to these people, who sometimes get out and commit another violent crime against our communities and neighborhoods.

The Reel Team aka THE DISRESPECT STOPPERS will make a difference in our communities and neighborhoods by enabling all truth seekers or young people and children to look to the team for moral support; it may be economical, mental or spiritual. The team will venture into the battle fields of injustice and darkness, a place where most people dare not explore. The team already knows going into battle with injustice and darkness will take everything they've got; blood, sweat and guts to defeat the enemy. The adrenaline rush from the team will inspire truth seekers to do something about fake thuggery, gun violence and crime and the adverse political climate they now live and work with in the 21st century protecting our communities and neighborhoods isn't a luxury. It's the duty of all truth seekers to join the Reel Team to help find the true solutions or help eradicate disrespect, hopelessness, dishonor and disunity out of our homes, schools and churches.

Mental and spiritual droughts have drained love, respect and good intentions to near critical levels in our communities and neighborhoods. Truth seekers are used to living and working with problems but now they are accumulating and reaching intolerable levels and everything indicates that the situation is going to get worse. Truth seekers must always remember the loser of Satan's disrespect games ends with someone leaking out the body, head or locked in chains of misery for life. No one ever wins while serving the angel named Lucifer aka Satan the devil, injustice and darkness. Truth seekers use to value the tranquility of our communities and neighborhoods now they are prisoners in their own homes because of fear of being robbed, murdered or raped while on the streets. As their communities and neighborhoods continue to collapse around them, they are forced to grasp what many people miss, the fragility of peace is dying and war is upon them.

The Reel Team aka THE DISRESPECT STOPPERS will be the new five star general or assassin who will not stop until injustice and darkness are finally eradicated from our homes, schools and churches. Injustice and darkness will no longer be pulling the strings behind the scenes manipulating our communities and neighborhoods into serving greed is good and hatred. Injustice and darkness continues to have our young people committing all these random, senseless and unnecessary shootings and killings. Our youth's lives continue to be sucked into the vacuum of injustice and darkness like carpet dirt and truth seekers continue to sit on the side line and let this genocide continue to happen without a fight from righteousness.

The Reel Team aka THE DISRESPECT STOPPERS will stand on any street corner ready and willing to recite or spread the gospel of Creation that GOOD WILL CONQUER EVIL AND LOVE WILL TRIUMPH OVER HATE and will teach our youth how to live life without injustice and darkness having a choke hold on their lives and to always remember without respect, love and good intentions there is no life, only death. The team will bring clarity to all the problems and find true solutions to why our communities, neighborhoods and our youths continue to live in the cesspool of injustice and darkness because most violent acts start out with a verbal confrontation or disagreement and when that does not work disrespect takes over and all the killing and shooting starts to take place.

The Reel Team aka THE DISRESPECT STOPPERS will always promote and sponsor serving love, respect and good intentions, it will help our youths to change their minds, bodies and souls, and start having respect for one another.

REEL TEAM ALWAYS KEEPING IT REAL!

THE REEL TEAM III
THE PUBLIC SERVICE MESSAGE
By
Mr. Dave R. Queeley

This is a PUBLIC SERVICE MESSAGE from THE REEL TEAM that they will take no prisoners of disrespect or violence alive. The Team message will be loud and clear and not just lip service. The Team has come to retrieve our communities, neighborhoods and government back from Satan's angels of destruction. The Reel Team will fire all incompetents and thieves who are now working in government or at the Police Station.

The Reel Team will become the new barometer of what's real or unreal in our communities, neighborhoods and government and they will be watching like a chicken hawk flying around looking for chickens or rats, so evil, sinful ways and disrespect will have to run and hide for fear of being eaten alive. Better communication and dialogue between decision makers, the police and the Reel Team will cement mutual trust and understanding about what went wrong with life in the Virgin Islands. It's now time to start searching for true solutions to all the problems that Virgin Islanders now face, young and old. As long as disrespect and violent behavior is young people's core interest or number one priority, they will never be able to handle disputes in a proper manner and life in the Virgin Islands will continue to get worse.

The Reel Team will work through the evil bureaucracy to shine a bright light on the sinister scheming of our greedy government officials or law enforcements officers who continue to conceal the corruption, fraud and abuse of power that has occurred in the past and continue today in the 21st century. In a very short time the Team will not worry about political or police consequences, all they will worry about is doing what is right for our communities and neighborhoods and that is government and police accountability. It's time for the police and politician to start doing everything possible to putting an end to all the unnecessary killing and shootings and start making plans to make things right within our communities and neighborhoods with true solutions that will solve the problem that seems illusory.

The Reel Team will remove disrespect and violence as an obstacle to the Creator's original plan of love, justice and good intentions and they will be working within the reality of change and respect. Disrespect and violence continue to contribute to the Demise of love, justice and good intentions because it wields great powers from the dark side and it's very demonic. The Reel Team will be the champion of respect, loyalty, and the undisputed heavy weight champion of reviving love, justice and good intention to its glory days of the past and they will not rest until the mission is accomplished. Returning to love, justice, and good intentions will be a landmark piece of legislation that is nearly a century in the making is long overdue. And it will take some time to see the full effects but it's a start to stopping the madness that disrespect and violence continue to cause.

Disrespect and violent behavior are now the new Bonnie and Clyde of the 21st century and serving evil, sinful ways and disrespect has a significant risk or failure because it's a never ending emotional roller coaster ride that leaves the rider uncertain whether They are up or down and there is no equal opportunity, just death.

The Reel Team will be stepping on the toes of all those people who continue to sell out to Satan's angels of destruction. The Reel Team message will be blunt and urgent it's time to revive love, justice and good intentions back into life in the VI. The Team will be open to anyone with an open mind who are truly willing and able to continue fighting the battle of "Good will conquer evil and Love will triumph over hate." All believers will see the Reel Team coming from a hundred miles away, to take back our communities, neighborhoods and government from sinful ways, evil and disrespect.

Our government officials have no business promoting or endorsing evil, sinful ways and disrespect. The same thing goes for law enforcement officers whose motto is, to protect and serve not divide and conquer. But lately they are not protecting much less serving. They are great at protecting evil, sinful ways and disrespect, but when it comes to serving love, justice and good intentions they are visionless.

Our government and police are now a political system that continues to forfeit public trust for Satan's bribes of destruction so he can continue to torpedo and sink our communities and neighborhoods into a spiritual and mental civil war. Remember they continue to join hands with Satan and his angels of destruction to continue oppressing the people of love, justice and good intention.

The Reel Team is all about loyalty and dedication to Good over Evil

THE REEL TEAM, KEEPING IT REAL!
REMEMBER THE MESSAGE
THE TRUTH WILL SPREAD
LIKE WILDFIRE

Reel Together Everyone Achieves More

THE CREATOR'S WORDS

By

Mr. Dave R. Queeley

There is nothing devious or crooked when it comes to the words of the CREATOR. It is plain to anyone with understanding and clear to those with knowledge of CREATION. Throughout the Bible scriptures, Christians are called to go public with their faith, love of CREATION and the words of wisdom. Faith in the CREATOR'S words must be expressed in words and deeds. In the Bible, faith is not something you possess, but rather something you practice. Christian believers have to put it into action or it really doesn't mean anything to the CREATOR. Becoming a Christian believer means identifying with the concerns, struggles and needs of non-believers around you.

CREATION is the gift that holds the words together because, "if you don't know the CREATOR, you will never know CREATION." Serving love, justice and good intentions needs BELIEVERS who are filled with the spirit of CREATION, which is LOVE NOT HATE. Hate is a scourge on the lives of Christians and a hindrance to entering the kingdom of CREATION'S peace, freedom and unity.

Christians who are dominated by sinful nature think only about sinful things. But those who are controlled by the CREATOR think about things that please the spirit of love, justice and good intentions. So letting sinful nature control your mind leads to self destruction and death, but letting the spirit of love, justice and good intentions control your mind leads to eternal life and peace with the CREATOR.

Jealousy, greed, selfishness and hate are not CREATION'S kind of wisdom. Such things are unearthly, unspiritual, and just plain demonic. Wherever there is jealousy, greed, selfishness and hate, Christian believers will find disorder and evil of all kinds. Biblical teaching and discipleship training are all part of learning the CREATOR'S words and the truth. CREATION'S words clearly teach that Christians are partners in the CREATOR'S mission of serving love, justice and good intentions. CREATION IS LOVE is a mission some Christians choose to ignore sometimes and try to forget that the CREATOR'S words are teaching of peace and love. CREATION wants BELIEVERS who care about the same thing, compassion and love, not hate. Serving love, justice and good intentions is a priceless treasure in CREATION'S eyes. Without the CREATOR'S words, love does not mean anything.

SHOW RESPECT FOR CREATION'S WORDS!

THE CREATOR'S WORDS II
By
Mr. Dave R. Queeley

THE CREATOR'S WORDS KNOWS NO BOUNDARIES!

The Bible AKA The Good Book strongly encourages all believers to pay attention to the CREATOR'S words and obey it to the fullest, and to become a living expression of CREATION'S words and love. Serving love, justice and good intentions demonstrates CREATIONS divine authority and power. The CREATOR'S love is not dead but right now it's on life support when it comes to believers loving CREATIONS words of wisdom. THE CREATOR'S love is the sound track to Christian living not greed, jealousy, hate, or selfishness. The CREATOR'S love is not going anywhere if you have faith and the words of wisdom in your life. True believers are the mouth piece of CREATION'S words and are chosen by the CREATOR to convey the message or teachings of love, justice and serving good intentions to the dark world of evil without being afraid of Satan the devil and hate.

 True believers are the people of the CREATOR and they are the church of love, justice and good intentions. They must remember Satan the devil and hate is on the prowl all the time to steal, conquer, and destroy it. Truth and love will triumph over evil and greed. True believers must always remember that non-believers are not the enemy, the angel whose name is Lucifer AKA Satan the devil. Non-believers now have the audacity to claim that the CREATOR'S love, justice and good intentions are dead, or that CREATION is no longer needed to survive in this sinful world of greed and hate.

Serving Lucifer AKA Satan the devil will lead believers to a GOD-less eternity of hate and selfishness. Many believers are slowly being backed into a corner by Lucifer and his angels of destruction and continue to forget that CREATION is love and not hate. If believers surrender to Lucifer and hate, they will surrender all of the biblical or historical faith of the first son of CREATION to Satan the devil that will destroy it. Most Christian believers are suffering from a bad case of amnesia by forgetting that, "For God so loved the world that he gave his only begotten son, who so ever believeth in him shall not perish but have everlasting life," John 3:16.

When believers conceal their love of CREATIONS words or keep it to themselves no one benefits from it, only Satan the devil and hate. Christian believers must never forget that non-believers continue to ask themselves this one question, "Why is it Christian Believers have no problem spreading gossip, injustice and hate, but have so much trouble spreading CREATION'S words of wisdom, love, and justice for all?" The CREATOR does not just give believers love; it defines the words of CREATION. Satan the devil will try to entrap believers with lies, evil, and hate; The CREATOR'S words leads believers to the truth and a peace of mind fulfilled with love and not hate.

The CREATOR' S love will purify all believers from sin and evil spirits, if they continue to believe. In the Bible AKA The Good Book in John 8:31-32 it says, "If you hold to my teaching you are really my disciples. Then you will know the truth and the truth will set you free." It's time all believers start speaking the CREATOR'S words and spreading love justice and good intentions with great boldness. The words of CREATION remain the same at all times, and that means the CREATOR will fulfill ALL.

TIME IS RUNNING OUT AND THE CREATORS WORDS WILL MAKE A DIFFERENCE!

P.S.   R.I.P. To all who died in the Virginia Tech Massacre…
4-17-2009 (1 YR ANNIVERSARY)

GONE BUT NOT FORGOTTEN, CREATION'S WORDS LIVE ON!

THE CHURCH
By
Mr. Dave R. Queeley

"NO MORE OF THE BLIND LEADING THE BLIND MENTALITY OR ATTITUDE."

The CHURCH is facing a crisis of historic proportions if respect, serving love, justice and good intentions does not return to the forefront of the mission. Some believers are now outraged and furious with the complete failure of CHURCH leadership in our communities and neighborhoods. Their view of the situation would be that they are led by incompetent believers who continue to be deceived by Satan's angels of destruction which are greed, jealousy, hate, and selfishness. Too many believers spent years or decades going to CHURCH and they still have not learned the laws of Creation or what it really means to serve love, justice, and good intention with their mind, body and soul without yielding to Satan's angels of destruction. Most Christians have forgotten that the CHURCH is suppose to be a hospital for the spiritually sick people who don't have a biblical understanding of Creation or the Creator's original plan of "Good will conquer evil and Love will triumph over hate."

There are a lot of inaccuracies associated with CHURCH and that the CHURCH has done a poor job of communicating to non-believers: that CHURCH is a place for people who are still on their spiritual journey. Non-believers continue to be skeptics about whether CHURCH, LOVE, JUSTICE AND GOOD INTENTIONS can once again regain its position as a world leader. The chorus of nay Sayers or non-believers who believe that the good old days for CHURCH, and serving love, justice have passed, have forgotten about the Holy Land where the son said, "I go to prepare a place for you" and "where I go that you may go also." This place is for them to dwell forever in love and harmony.

CHURCH is a direct message to all so call Christians who go to CHURCH on Sundays. PLEASE STOP disrespecting the Creator when you say to yourself on Sundays, "I'm going to CHURCH," that means you're here for the ALPHA and OMEGA, the beginning and the end. Christians when you go to CHURCH, PLEASE STOP making plans to do the Creator wrong. Mr. Realistic is going to tell all Christians FOUR FACTS that do not lie!

FACT ONE: "Watching the Clock" Christians you've got six days to serve darkness, but you can't sit still for two hours to hear the words of Creation. Remember Philippians C4V13 says "I can do all things through Christ which strengthen me." Not SOME things but ALL things.

FACT TWO: "Parents who don't discipline their kids" CHURCH is suppose to be Holy Ground so parents need to do a better job when it comes to taking care of their kids on Holy Ground, because it's not a play ground. "Spare the rod, spoil the child."

FACT THREE: "Not pay attention to the words of Creation" Meaning gossiping, criticizing and all that complaining must stop and one must start living as examples of the Creator's words.
FACT FOUR: "CHURCH is not a fashion show, strip club, or the mall" It's a place to worship the Creator in truth and right and most of all good over evil and love over hate.
"Rend your heart not your garment."

It's time CHURCH removed all obstacles that impede believers on their Christian journey of spreading the good news that the Creator is love and not hate. Isolating the evil element and spirit that has been controlling CHURCH for so many centuries, it's a hard thing to do because there are so many closet devil worshippers coming to CHURCH on Sundays trying to deceive the Creator into thinking that they love Creation.

CHURCH is now caught up in a web of hate, adultery and destruction, because Christians are now too busy rustling through the airport of greed, disrespect and material bondage that they forget to

stop and give the Creator true praise as the Creator of all things
SEEN AND UNSEEN.

Christians must realize, to continue serving evil sinful ways and
disrespect, is like going into CHURCH on Sunday and the priest
says everybody go home and have a party, because Jesus has now
sided with the Devil and evil has conquered good and believers
know that's a lie.

CHURCH II
By
Mr. Dave R. Queeley

The Creator has given all believers a CODE OF LAWS and has designed a place at which they are to worship and it's called CHURCH. It's time the CHURCH comfort our communities and neighborhoods with the truth about the good news that the Creator's Kingdom of Love, Justice and Good Intentions is the real Government, that will bring an end to all evil, wickedness and disrespect that continue to run rampant. It will transform our communities and neighborhoods back into a paradise of honor, loyalty and respect for the Creator's words of wisdom. Believers must always remember no CHURCH has a monopoly on moral truth only the Creator has that monopoly.

The CHURCH has lost its vision about what it's suppose to represent which is to always spread the Good News that the Creator is love and not hate. It's time CHURCH start doing its job which is "to seek the lost and lead them to the son (Christ), the one who can save them ", Matthew C6V33. Christians now have a religious culture whose focus is not on the Creator's words of wisdom. But on Satan's angels of destruction which are greed, jealously, hate and most of all selfishness, The CHURCH is falling apart for the same reason people do they are imperfect because nothing is perfect on EARTH, the only thing that is perfect is the LOVE of Creation.

The CHURCH possessed great wealth and political power, so if the CHURCH returns to love, justice and good intentions as it's full time job it will usher in a new era of prosperity for honor, loyalty and having respect that will become a major player on the world stage like evil, sinful ways and disrespect which continue to wreak havoc on their communities and neighborhoods.

All around CHURCH, Christians are carelessly ignoring the Creator's words and warnings and some Christians have forgotten about what the Bible AKA The Good Book says the first commandment is, "HAVE NO OTHER GODS BEFORE ME."

Christians often face hateful circumstances and are not immune from the traumas or tragedies of life because Satan the Devil is always around the corner ready to persecute believers who have lost faith in Creation or the Creator's words of wisdom.

Living in sin or darkness has blinded some Christians for so long they forget why they were baptized, "The water was not to make you wet but to dry out the heart mind and soul of all evil, sinful ways and disrespect and most of all to wash out hate out of the temple of Creation.

Christians must always remember "Baptism symbolizes a person's decision to disown him or herself and to be owned instead by the Creator and the words of wisdom and to have a clear conscience about the Creator's original plan. It's time for quality presentation of the Creator's words in our communities and neighborhoods. The CHURCH has now become a place where people with money and power believe they can buy their way out of sin or darkness or buy their way into heaven but they keep on forgetting it's easier for a camel to go through the eye of a needle, that for a rich man to take his riches to heaven.

STORE YOUR RICHES IN HEAVEN NOT ON EARTH OR IN CHURCH, BUT IN HEAVEN

CHURCH III
By
Mr. Dave R. Queeley

No more diluting of the truth, so here comes the truth. No matter who hates or love it because the truth has authority and power.

Church has now become watered down, ineffective and departed from helping those people who are desperately in need of a mental and spiritual renovation. They use to be the originators of all that was good in our communities and neighborhoods now their new principles are disunity, disloyalty and selfishness which are now their top priority, not the Creator's original plan or the laws of Creation.

The Church was once a leader of love, respect and good intentions but now it's being diluted by evil doers and non believers. These people are always working against the building or returning to having respect, love, and good intentions in life because they don't have any use for the Creator's original plan or the Laws of Creation in their lives. The Church continues to take in billions of dollars year after year, while their communities and neighborhoods continue to suffer from lack of mental and spiritual guidance. It's now the biggest business on planet earth where greed and selfishness is now the boss.

The Bible aka The Good Book talks about Church in Matthew C21V13, it says "and said unto them it is written, my house shall be called the house of prayer, but ye have made it a den of thieves." Its well knowledge that back in the good old days, the Church was a place of generosity, caring and peace and it reflected the positive light of love, respect and good intentions. Evil doers and non believers continue to think going to Church is often seen as secondary and not even a vital part of their mental and spiritual life. They are not satisfied with organized religion because they continue to feel they are not getting anything from Church mentally or spiritually; just giving up their money. They feel people in Church were judging each other yet they are doing some of the same things evil doers and non believers are doing, so they stop going because they feel there is hypocrisy in Church and it they keep going they would become hypocrites.

The Church is now mainly a political machine, not a place of worship anymore because they are mixing in politics and wars of the world into their business. While still so many believers are UNEDUCATED about the Creator's original plan and the Laws of Creation. Church has lost the strong identity of the good old days when love, respect and good intentions ruled. Now they have become a dwelling place of thieves, demons and criminals where true love, respect and good intentions are now hard to find. It's like looking for a needle in a haystack. Any moral authority and credibility the Church had in the past, the good old days has now been destroyed by greed, hatred, selfishness and corruption.

The need for reform is now urgent because there are now anonymous sources in the Church who continue to peddle bogus information about the Creator's original plan and the Laws of Creation and they will be exposed in the future when love, respect and good intentions takes back the Church. It will stop the traffic of falsehoods, the imaginary conspiracies by the angel named Lucifer aka Satan and his Angels of Destruction that has been running rampant for a while in believers' lives. Reality has retreated and fantasy continues to advance to god like status because believers are succumbing to the falsehoods and belief of Satan and his Angels of Destruction. If this continues to happen the good old days are not coming back; when love, respect and good intentions was Church highest and top priority on the battle field of Good over Evil.

Church is now composed of people who do not have faith or the spiritual vision to do what it takes to become a Christian. Most Churches have departed from the doctrine that was given unto the Church by the only begotten son and the apostles. They need to start doing a better job of doing the Creator's work which is to seek the lost and lead them to the first born of Creation, the one who can save them. Churches are supposed to be a welcoming and caring place for the spiritually and mentally sick, but they don't treat believers like that anymore. It's now all about how much money you can put in the collection envelope or basket. Instead of using the Church as their anchor or pillar in the battle of Good over Evil, they use it for all the wrong reasons to make money, the root of all evil.

Truth seekers are in danger since losing control of the Church. Since greed, hatred, selfishness and corruption continue to be religious leaders' number one priority. It's time for religious leaders to be more specific about their plans, how they are going to jump start the return to having respect, love, and good intentions in their communities and neighborhoods as an everyday activity. Love, respect and good intentions can be found in any Church that has the Creator's original plan and the Laws of Creation as its foundation. Back in the good old days, the Church on the corner was a sign of the presence of the Creator in the community and neighborhood. It did not represent big business or a money making machine. The Church is supposed to be one nation under Creation, nothing else.

The truth is TA also known as TOP AUTHORITY!

DEAR JOU'VERT
By
Mr. Dave R. Queeley

Dear Jou'vert,

It's a shame that once again, you have become the casualty of gun violence and street justice. These attitudes and actions now have changed everything from bad to worse. It's a shame young people and children have such easy access to all kinds of guns, like going to footlocker.

2013 Jou'vert was another black eye to the VI once again. So many people spent thousands of dollars, to come and enjoy the pinnacle of Carnival, which is Jou'vert. Nine bands on the road ready to play music, and once again fake thuggery has spoiled the party with shots fired and three people injured. These fake thugs keep on forgetting when the settlers let Carnival happen, it was the only time of the year our ancestors could have celebrated African heritage. Jou'vert origins coincide with the emancipation from physical slavery, when former slaves could openly celebrate their African heritage in the streets; after centuries of mocking their masters in backyard masquerade balls and parties, hidden far out of sight of the settlers. So it's time to start giving Jou'vert enough respect and love from now on moving deeper and deeper into the 21st century of the unknown.

In the 21st century fake thuggery continues to wreck the so-called freedom of expression that the settlers gave our ancestors centuries ago. In the VI, this freedom of expression is only 61 years young, making 62 in 2014. I hope Jou'vert can reach the Carnival finish line. VIPD, it will be unfair to our ancestors to cancel Jou'vert because only then the criminal element will start celebrating that they shut down Jou'vert for good. In 2013, VIPD disrespected our ancestors of the 1733 revolt, by not having Jou'vert on St. John.

Jou'vert brings people from all over the world and all of the

Caribbean, to come and party with us, but fake thuggery keeps on giving Carnival and Jou'vert a bad name and black eye once again. Jou'vert never hurt anyone; it's the one love tramp up the road. So in 2014, all you fake thugs stay the bleep home, because we want to party in 2014.

Thank you very much for your time. We the people love you Jou'vert!

Thanks for listening.

COLORED RELATIONSHIPS
By
Mr. Dave R. Queeley

Unconditional love is hard to find in the 21st century. From the beginning of time there was true love, honor and loyalty between the Colored Male and Female. Now in the 21st century Colored Males and Females have lost respect for one another. Colored Males and Females need to learn to communicate even when love hurts and be mature enough to understand that sex isn't the only instant pleasure.

Great communication can also be instant pleasure too: Colored Males and Females must understand the concept of teamwork and getting through rough patches in their relationship. Together as one and must remember love, respect and joy is always spontaneous, never scheduled and the perfection of love, respect and joy is a long process, it's not an overnight thing.

Secrets, drama, and jealousy are the main stumbling blocks that continue to prevent Colored Males and Females from advancing to the oneness of two people seeking a partnership that will stand the test of time like Creation.

In a relationship today, some Colored Females will experience domestic violence over their lifetime. It could be physical or verbal abuse, this is not acceptable behavior by Colored Males because it goes against the Creator's original plan of "Good will conquer evil and Love will triumph over hate." Not having love, justice and good intentions continue to lead to domestic squabbles or fights that sometimes leads to life in prison or death.

Ups and downs are the growing pains of a relationship maturing. But Colored Males and Females must remember it's not easy maintaining a relationship based on love, justice and good intentions and it takes a lot of time and respect and they have to be mature enough to understand and know that anything worthwhile requires effort, hard work and lots of sacrifice, if they want their relationship to last a long time or not end up in divorce court.

Colored Males and Females now need years of therapy to understand the demons that are causing them to sabotage their own happiness. Cultural recovery of love, justice and good intentions should be their number one priority and not hate because the Creator is love.

Colored Males and Females need to follow their inner compass to create a relationship far beyond any standard set by established society and they must always remember serving love, justice and good intentions should be a prerequisite for having a relationship with one another. In the 21st century love, justice and good intentions should never be a babbler like disrespect and violent behavior, the number one relationship wrecker. When the element of respect is lost, there is a possibility for miscommunication and for things to run amuck.

It's time Colored Males start respecting and listening without judgment or condemnation to the Colored Female, because she knows what's best for Creation. There is great strength and energies in the Colored Female and the Colored Male must use it to the best of their ability to love, respect and leave behind the lifestyle of immorality and idolatry if they want to survive or have a relationship with the GREATEST WOMAN ALIVE for another 5 centuries. A true relationship is hard to find.

TIME TO REMOVE THE VEIL OF SELF DECEPTION AND SEEK LOVE AND RESPECT.

LOVE IS NOT A GAME!

I GOT

By
Mr. Dave R. Queeley

I GOT my criminal degree from the University of Bovoni also known as The Creeps (B. V. D.), now in the 21st century, it's called The Guzzle. This university is where I learned all the evil tricks and trades of the angel named Lucifer, also known as Satan the devil world of hatred. I did things I sometimes want to forget or never talk about because at that time of my life I was really under Satan's authority. He was in full control of my life and destiny, in and out of jail and prison like it was a game.

I GOT my high school diploma from I. E. K. H. S. (Ivanna Eudora Kean High School). It took more than four years because I was always in trouble in school, because I did not want to follow the rules. I am an alumni of the Juvenile Delinquency Police Program also known as J. D. P. P., been there done that. Nuff respect to police officer Hubert Rumbo, he was from someplace in the U. S. A. I cannot say where. I GOT two teachers that really made a difference in my life for real. They were Miss Freda Smith, a math teacher who is now resting in peace. I want to say THANK YOU. And Ms. Tulip Fleming, the English, Speech and Drama teacher. In her class is where I found my talent for writing and speaking. It was a place of peace of mind from the evil activities I was involved with on school grounds.

What I GOT is a message for all young people and children. If you compare your mind to a blank piece of paper, tell me what you get? The answer is, if you do not write anything on the paper, you got nothing on it; just like your mind, if you do not put anything in its got nothing in it.
Since I started seeking and serving truth and honor, I have obtained these degrees of life...

I GOT a Bachelor in the Art in Keeping It Real, a Master's Degree of Respect, Understanding and Loyalty and a Doctorate in Love,

Respect, Justice and Good Intentions. All mental and spiritual degrees that keep me well educated while on the job of spreading the Creator's original plan and laws of creation as an everyday activity to the young people and children who continue to live fast and die young, going deeper and deeper into the century of the unknown. In the 21st century I can now be called an in-depth person and writer whose inter-reaction of life, love, justice and good intentions, recalls the simplicity of the old-time spirituals and spirits of doing what's right and positive in life.

In the fields of injustice, evil and darkness,I GOT my early experience as an in-depth person to become a writer. My writings are the living words and works of good intentions and the Creator. It's not just for the privileged few, but for all people. Especially the ones who remain in mental and spiritual captivity. I will always write exactly what I see wrong with society. Whoever wants to make me the enemy instead of a friend, go ahead, I don't care, the Creator got my back at all times. It's never too late, a man or woman can change their mind, bodies and souls; but the Creator's mission for life remains the same, which is GOOD OVER EVIL.

TRY IT, IT WORKS!
I'VE GOT IT!

SUPERSTARS
Dedicated to DJ Avalanche
By
Mr. Dave R. Queeley

"It's time to bury the mentally and spiritually dead now."

Mental and spiritual SUPERSTARS are not born from evil hype and myths. They are born from hard work and achievements that lead to success you can't manufacture, buy and sell at no time in life. The time has come for the bandwagon of greed, hatred and disrespect to start shrinking as We the People keep moving forward into the 21st century of the unknown. It does not matter that greed, hatred and disrespect's occupation of some people's minds, bodies and souls has no end in sight. But real SUPERSTARS motto in the battle of good intentions over evil will always be "NO RETREAT, NO SURRENDER TO GREED, HATRED AND DISRESPECT." We the People have to start operating like an Air Force fighter plane and start dropping bombs on greed, hatred and disrespect, trying very hard to get rid of them out of our communities and neighborhoods. These evil feelings, attitudes and actions should never be in anyone's rearview mirror of life at any time.

Greed, hatred and disrespect has turned some people into today's hypocrites who continue to play Russian roulette with their lives on a regular basis. If this continues to happen, there will not be any more mental and spiritual superstars who are willing to be a part of the ERADICATION SQUAD. These people who are a part of the eradication squad knows it's their duty and responsibility to promote and support the Creators original plan and laws of creation so that respect, love and good intentions for one another can be a part of everyone's lives while moving forward into the battle of good intentions over evil spirits at all times. Respect, love and good intentions for one another will be the executioner of all evil and negative personas that continues to define some people's lifestyle.

Negative and evil personas keep these same people from becoming mental and spiritual superstars who are working to see good intentions become successful and victorious in the battle with evil spirits in the future. The best assessment of these same people is that they have sold their mind, body and soul to the angel named Lucifer, also known as Satan the devil and don't give a damn if good intentions lives or dies in the battle with evil spirits. They keep on forgetting there is no space in between evil spirits and good intentions; it's one or the other. Real mental and spiritual superstars know this. That's why they are always on the side of good intentions in the battle for world supremacy, making sure the eradication squad is victorious in the future. Not being on the side of good intentions is the ultimate betrayal to the creator's original plan which is, "Good will conquer evil and Love will triumph over hate." These people who are not on the side of good intentions, keep on forgetting without following the laws of creation, they will continue to be turned into mental and spiritual savages and never mental and spiritual superstars.

They keep on forgetting that love, respect and good intentions for one another used to be the universal language that everyone all around the world used to speak to one another. Now in the 21st century, we don't speak this language very much anymore; they do not have any vision of good conquering evil and love triumphing over hate in their lives. They continue to speak the foreign language of being greedy and disrespectful people to one another as the days on earth gets shorter. They keep on forgetting the time has come to burn down the evil empire of greed that continues to lead them astray and have some of them at times saying "bleep the Creators original plan and laws of creation without any apology.

They keep on forgetting that the maintenance of the covenant of love, respect and good intentions for one another in its entirety is the first step of anyone who wants to become a mental and spiritual superstar who has the spirit of righteous and will soar to new heights of inspiration, courage and respect that will always be involved in love, respect and good intentions for one another, because it always leads to an invitation to the party of seeking and serving truth and honor.

SUPREME LOVE
By
Mr. Dave R. Queeley

The Creator's Love is now mired in mediocrity and our community now needs help enforcing the laws of creation because supreme love is long overdue.

It's uplifting, often difficult and is an essential emotion to setting our community free from the angel named Lucifer aka Satan the Devil.

It has undisputed clout and must become the number one force that works against the servants of Satan the Devil and hate.

Creator's Love is not just a luxury for the chosen few but a luxury for all truth seekers who truly know their supreme being.

It should be the supreme ruler of the universe and our dying communities and neighborhoods.
It shows truth seekers the significance of the Bible's prophecies that will be fulfilled in the future.

The Creator's Love will bring an end to all wickedness and transform our communities and neighborhoods into a paradise of righteousness that promote and support truth and honor all day, every day.

It knows no color and it is non-political and it adheres to the Bible as its only authority.

This authority does not bear the marks of fiction because it's always for real.

And it does not show partiality because the Supreme Being is love and not hate.

The Creator's Love has evaporated from the lives of truth seekers because everywhere you look you see Satan the Devil and hate continue to run things without a fight from righteousness.

The Creator's Love will set truth seekers free from the emotional bondage of hate because Satan is the emotional tyranny of destruction and only the Creator's Love can save truth seekers from spiritual disaster. No one has love greater and unconditional like the Creator. Satan the Devil and hate is only a cheap duplicate.

The Creator's Love is too powerful to be diluted by selfishness, jealousy, hate and most of all greed.

It has a standard of excellence by which all truth seekers will be measured for all eternity.
And it knows no limit to its endurance, no end to its trust.

The Creator's Love stands when all else has fallen. Remember the Creator's Love is supreme love that rules and will never be fictitious.

SUPREME LOVE II
By
Mr. Dave R. Queeley

The Creator's Love will always be superior to Satan the Devil and hate, no matter how hard evil or sin tries to be number one or the light of the world. In the Bible aka the Good Book it says, "Satan himself keeps transforming himself into an angel of light." 2 Corinthians 11:14.

The Creator's Love is still number one and superior over all of Satan's vanity.

And it's the defender of individual rights, loyalty and justice and not evil and disrespect.

With the Creator's Love there is no limitation to what believers can accomplish in the battle of Good will conquer evil and Love will triumph over hate.

It does not judge truth seekers by the color of their skin or character.

It only judges truth seekers by their deeds and thoughts.

In the Creator's Love, truth seekers will not experience disappointments. Disappointments only come from serving the angel named Lucifer aka Satan the Devil whose motto is to steal, conquer and continue to destroy and divide.

The Creator's Love can cure the lawlessness, disrespect and the disunity that plagues our communities and neighborhoods.

It comes in all shapes and sizes and all truth seekers who share it are very lucky because they have a hold around them from being tempted by Satan the Devi. They must remember Satan will always be just an imposter or scam artist when it comes to serving love, respect and good intentions.

As servants of love, respect and good intentions truth seekers must not let Satan's agents of destruction which are greed, jealousy, hate and selfishness continue to undermine their loyalty to the Creator's Love.

The Creator's Love must represent all righteousness and superior acts in the world today.

It's not like money, "earning it is very hard and losing it is very easy."

The Creator's Love will never have any interruptions.

IT'S FOREVER!

SUPREME LOVE III
By
Mr. Dave R. Queeley

The Creator's love specializes in things that are impossible and it touches believer's lives in a special way that Satan, the Devil can never do. The Creator's love will always represent patience, kindness and loyalty.

The Creator's love is a confidence builder and is a life changing experience and not a bad predicament like serving Satan, the Devil and hate.

The Creator's love and justice come to those who are prepared to fight for it and on this mission, everyone is equal, no one is above the law and there is no escape, however famous, talented or rich you are, you must do your part to make sure "good conquer evil and love triumph over hate."

The Creator's love understands believers thinking and emotions better than they do and he knows what pathways they should avoid.

The Creator's love is never a source of wickedness only Satan, the Devil who is the King Pin of wickedness.

The Creator's love is the King of Eternity and it will end all suffering and injustice.

The Creator's love is the only invisible power that believers now need in their life not greed, disrespect, or selfishness.

The Creator's love has no string of unrighteousness attached to it. The Creator's love has no complication or frustration only a peace of mind.

The Creator's love is never disrespectful. It's always obedience. Serving the Creator's love is an opportunity to unplug evil, sinful ways and disrespect from our communities, neighborhoods, and the lives of all young people.

The Creator's love will never abandon believers if they remain loyal to his words of wisdom.

The Creator's love will help all believers overcome political, racial or the economical barriers that continue to divide them. The Creator's love is the foundation of life, justice, love and serving good.

THE CREATOR'S LOVE DOES NOT SHOW FAVORITISM.

Written by
Mr. Dave Queeley
2009

PERFECT LOVE
By
Mr. Dave R. Queeley

The Mother's love is the only perfect love from the cradle to the grave.

It's the ground zero in the fight against evil, injustice and darkness.

The Mother's love has a monopoly on morality.

And it's never disgraceful or oppressed. It's always there no matter what happens good or bad in life.

The Mother's love is the greatest role model.

It is never partial.

The Mother's love is an energy or feeling that can never be broken.

And it's never deceitful. It's always honest.

The Mother's love is always food for the soul and never phony or artificial.

It's a courage that never surrenders, it always moves forward.

And it's never unfaithful. It's always loyal.

The Mother's love is transparent. It sees no color.

The Mother's love is the only accurate knowledge of the truth and honor.

Evil spirits or hatred cannot separate truth seekers from the Mother's Love.

Hell hath no fury like the Mother's love when truth seekers are scorned.

The Mothers love is always straightforward and will never be a double crosser.

The Mother's love never sleeps. It's always awake to fight evil sinful ways and hate.

THE MOTHER'S LOVE!

PERFECT LOVE II
By
Mr. Dave R. Queeley

The MOTHER'S LOVE is always a source of mental and spiritual strength and encouragement.

The MOTHER'S LOVE speaks the truth all day long, no matter what happens good or bad in life.

And it's never bitter sweet; it's the only form of real true love and respect.

It will never lose its temper; it's always under control.

The MOTHER'S LOVE is a tie that binds the mind, body and soul forever.

It is a true melting pot and its everlasting.

And it's never in denial about hopelessness, greed, dishonor, and disunity.

The MOTHER'S LOVE is the number one authority on teaching respect, love, understanding and good intentions.

Because it's pure and undefiled. The MOTHER'S LOVE is a fearless as any pirate that sailed the high seas.

It's always unconditional.

And it is never fool's gold.

The MOTHER'S LOVE is like a diamond, it has many different sides to it.

And it will help the mission of life to be accomplished which is "Good will conquer evil and Love will triumph over hate."

The MOTHER'S LOVE is the Alpha and the Omega of having respect, love and good intentions as the top and highest priority in life.

The MOTHER'S LOVE will be waiting on truth seekers on judgment day.

Believe it or not she will be waiting there!

FOR PARENTS ONLY
SUPREME LOVE OVER SATAN THE DEVIL AND HATE
By
Mr. Dave R. Queeley

The PARENTS that prepare their children for the mission of good over evil in the world will equip them to obey rather than simply to know the Creators words of wisdom, getting ready for this mission of good over evil means PARENTS have to repent and start turning around from Satan's dead end ways of living that will end up getting them killed eternally. PARENTS are suppose to be ambassadors of love and peace to our communities and neighborhoods not Satan the Devil and hate because their presence is to slow down the corrosion and spoiling effects of evil and to reinforce the message that peaceful co-existence, cooperation and communication are keys to helping complete the mission of "Good will conquer evil and Love will triumph over hate."

PARENTS will need to show with actions not just words, that the mission can be achieved. PARENTS need to become the new agents of change and light to the darkness and confused world of our children in the 21st century. Old sinful ways and evil patterns are broken and a new freedom in the Creator's words of wisdom will be experienced without fear of Satan the Devil and hate. PARENTS must decide what price they are willing to pay to save our children from becoming another statistical teenage pregnancy, murder victim, or someone charged with using an unauthorized firearm during the commission of a violent crime of hate.

PARENTS should be blamed for not teaching their children about the mission or bible from an early age. Back in the good old days children went to church every Sunday and one day out of the week there was bible study by someone's house. In the 21st century my quote, "The bible has taken the place of pornography and pornography has taken the place of the bible." Meaning pornography was taboo and the bible was everywhere, in life now the bible is taboo and pornography is everywhere, because sex sells everything.

 PARENTS are now afraid to raise their children with respect, discipline, and honor because of all those child abuse laws tying their hands from disciplining their children. In the bible it says, "Spare the rod spoil the child," the rod of correction has disappeared from our children's lives that are why PARENTS continue to see the blood bath every day of the week on the streets of their communities and neighborhoods. Satan the Devil and hate continue to use our children as human shields in the battle of evil over good.

PARENTS must now work together at 100 miles per hour to get rid of all Satan's angels of destruction, which are greed, jealousy, hate, and selfishness. They must never forget about his new angels of destruction in the 21st century, they are the inter-net and satellite televisions, which are in millions of PARENT'S homes with children who are left home alone with Satan's new angels of destruction to raise them.

PARENTS must realize the decision to start serving love, justice and good intentions should reassure them that their children will be protected from indecent material on the nation's airways or the blood bath that Satan the Devil and hate still continue to control.

PARENTS must start explaining to their children that when love, justice, serving good intentions conquer our communities and neighborhoods the blood bath will stop forever.

In the 21st century this statement should be PARENTS motto:

LOVE is the SKIES, JUSTICE is the EARTH, and SERVING GOOD is the SEA.

FOR PARENTS ONLY II
NO BENDING
By
Mr. Dave R. Queeley

Inspired by Mr. Sokoto Clendinen

Many PARENTS seem to believe that good parenting means bending to the will of their children. That's not good parenting. Children need to learn life is not a spa treatment, it's full of ups and downs and you do not always get what you want. In the 21st century PARENTS need to be held accountable for raising and educating their children and stop letting Satan the devil and hate do their job as a parent.

PARENTS must teach love, justice and serving good intentions because it's an opportunity to impact the lives of their children, and to help them achieve their dreams and fulfill their Creative potential that they have the power to destroy Satan the devil and be agents of change in their communities and neighborhoods. PARENTS cannot continue to take a cosmetic approach to erecting evil ways, Satan, and greed out of their children's lives.

PARENTS must realize there is no substitute for spending time with their children because Creations greatest gift to a man and woman is a child. PARENTS can't pick or choose which pieces of Satan or evil they want to keep in their children's lives, while selfishness continues to choke their children to death. By watching television or the internet most children already believe that by serving Satan the devil and hate their future will be lined with streets of gold but they keep on forgetting that serving Satan the devil and hate is like dropping money into a slot machine in Las Vegas (SIN CITY), it does not pay off, often you lose more than you win.

PARENTS must explain the painful and dark details of serving evil or hate to their children who continue to live without morals. Our children will change only when PARENTS do, and when they stop promoting evil ways. Serving love, justice and good intentions is a symbol of the determination of PARENTS to free their children from the oppression of Satan the devil and his agents of destructions which are greed, hate, jealousy and selfishness and for them to enjoy the fruits of respect, honor, and loyalty.

PARENTS must teach their children to never look in the rear view mirror of life because they will never need what's behind them only what's coming at them in the future. They must realize that success in life depends on a great education and the current and future work force will demand that you have a degree beyond a high school diploma. PARENTS must always remember serving love, justice and good intentions is a path-way out of evil ways or selfishness; it is what their ancestors worked, fought and died for Good will conquer evil and Love will triumph over hate.

PARENTS must teach their children in the 21st century, TO KNOW THSELF; TO BE THYSELF AND TO LOVE THYSELF. There are mountains of hate and many rivers of evil that continues to run through their children's lives with no end in sight and PARENTS continue to do nothing about it!

PARENTS ITS TIME TO BREAK DOWN ALL THE EVIL BARRIERS AND UPHOLD THE HONOR AND DIGNITY OF PARENTING.

NO MORE BENDING PARENTS

FOR PARENTS ONLY III
By
Mr. Dave R. Queeley

TELLING IT LIKE IT IS, NO SUGAR COATING, JUST KEEPING IT REAL WITH PARENTS

PARENTS must stay focused on the goal of teaching their children how to become the new soldiers of righteousness on the battlefield of disrespect and violent behavior and that's no easy task in the 21st century.

PARENTS need to explain and show by examples exactly what it means to be a responsible adult. Their examples will be the most powerful way to help their children to see the important values of having responsible behavior. If PARENTS continue to forever shield their children from the difficulties of life, they may in fact be stunting their ability to take on life's challenges in a positive way. Disrespect and violent behavior continue to be the number one set back to their children's future of continuing the battle of "Good will conquer evil and Love will triumph over hate."

PARENTS have become the new disrespect and violent behavior watchdog, never it's partner because children learn from what they see their parents do, so if adults continue to SETTLE DISAGREEMENTS IN A VIOLENT MANNER their children will think the way to settle their DISAGREEMENTS by reacting violently. PARENTS have failed spectacularly at doing their job of raising responsible adults because IMPERFECT PARENTS cannot produce perfect offspring.

Returning to love, justice, and good intentions will stoke a new confidence in parents to see the Creator's original plan accomplished and they will not stop until disrespect and violence is gone forever and their lives can go back to normal like back in the good old days when people, young and old had respect for one another. PARENTS have to demand the Democratic and Republican Parties have to fully invest in their children's educational future, they have to create an economic opportunity if they truly want to see a decline in murder, rapes, or assaults. They continue to offer no immediate remedies or long-term solution to fighting the problem of disrespect and violent behavior, before it gets worse. It's now bad and if all the unnecessary killing and shooting continue their landscape will resemble Sudan or Rwanda in the future.

PARENTS, Government officials and law enforcement officers have been powerless in stopping the leaking of blood and body fluids that continues gushing from their children on the streets of their communities and neighborhoods. All the unnecessary killings and shootings has raised doubts about PARENTS, Government officials, and Law enforcement officers trying to stop the flow of blood and body fluids that continue to run like a river in the streets of disrespect or in the Valleys of Hate. PARENTS must remember their children's communities and neighborhoods are now based on crime, slaughter, and dishonor, not love, justice, and good intentions.

PARENTS must always remember the evaporation of respect, love, justice, and good intentions continue to be the number one source of death to their children's future!
PARENTS do not want to hear they should be cultivating humanity, self-discipline and respect in their homes, school and churches. They now need to be guided by this biblical scripture, "TRAIN A CHILD IN THE WAY HE SHOULD GO AND WHEN HE IS OLD HE WILL NOT TURN FROM IT." Prov. C22V6. PARENTS are supposed to be the Guardian of Obedience to the Creator's words of wisdom.

If PARENTS return to love, justice and good intentions it will re-ignite their children to start spreading the good news of the Creator's original plan of Good will conquer evil and Love will triumph over hate" and it will help rejuvenate their communities and neighborhoods and all young people to having respect for Creation. PARENTS have now risen a generation of children who does not know what having respect means, and they NOW know about violent behavior and disrespect, and it's an epidemic on the streets and PARENTS continue ignoring it.

PARENTS must teach their children in the 21st century about Aretha Franklin's RESPECT and they should always know and remember…

RESPECT, YOU CANT BUY IT, YOU CAN'T MAKE IT, AND YOU SURE CAN'T FAKE IT.

YOU EITHER HAVE IT
OR
YOU DON'T HAVE IT.

FOR PARENTS ONLY
STOP PLAYING

FOR PARENTS ONLY IV
Back To The Basics
By
Mr. Dave R. Queeley

It's time for all parents to get back to the real basics of parenting. The basics of parenting are to teach children and young people about having respect, love, and good intentions for one another as their highest priority in their lives. Children and young people are sponges, they soak up everything they see and hear, negative and positive. If children and young people see their parents disrespecting themselves or solving problems violently, they will think that's the right way to live their lives or to act in the public.

It's time for parents to teach their children and young people about the Creator's original plan and the Laws of Creation before they take one more step down hell's path of eternal fire and continue to spiral out of control. Parents must realize children and young people are now dying because of their disobedience to the Creator's original plan and the Laws of Creation.

Some parents are to be blames and need to be held accountable for juvenile delinquents because when their children are babies, they used obscenities and degrading expressions to express authority and sometimes love and respect. These behaviors by parents are all factors that contribute to juvenile delinquency. YOU REAP WHAT YOU SOW. So if parents continue sowing disrespect, violent behavior, dishonor, and disunity that's what you will reap: never having respect, love, and good intentions for one another because those seeds were not sowed.

Parents must work hard towards making it impossible for their children and young people to go to prison or jail so it will not hinder their future success because society is really harder on people who go to the pit of doom and justice (jail or prison) and come back out. Parents must remember the basics of parenting is being an inspiration to their children and young people to be an inspiration they have to start setting better examples for their children and young people to follow. Tell them the truth without sugar coating the facts because in the 21st century they now want instant gratification not hard work.

Children and young people are growing up fast in a very different world from the one their parents use to know. Now it's all about cyber space, text message, face book, emails, twitter, and you tube. They are all a part of the introduction to Satan's artificial intelligence that will try to take over the world and rule like a communist dictator. In the 21st century Satan and his Angels of Destruction has deceived and blinded some parents to the precious truth found in the Creator's original plan, words and the Laws of Creation. So if they are deceived and blinded to the truth their children and young people will grow up being deceived and blinded to the truth and they sometimes end up in the pit of injustice and doom (jail or prison) for a very long time.

Parents need to start sponsoring and promoting the children and young people who have not crossed over and picked up a gun and committed a violent crime. In the 21st century a lot of parents are without the proper knowledge and parenting skills and have the inability to teach their children and young people about the Creator's original plan and Laws of Creation. Young people and children need to hear the message of positivity and self empowerment that will raise awareness about all the social issues that affect them and continue to lead them astray from the Creator's original plan and the Laws of Creation.

All parents must remember the original plan which is GOOD WILL CONQUER EVIL AND LOVE WILL TRIUMPH OVER HATE. This must be spread like wildfires burning in children and young people lives. Parents have forgotten that children and young people do not come with warranties, so you can't take them back to where you got them from; you've got to deal with it. Back in our ancestor days, parents and grandparents use to have a moral responsibility of teaching their children or grandchildren about the Creator's original plan and about the true Laws of Creation. Now in the 21st century the internet and TV are the ones teaching moral responsibility and respect; that's no good at all for our future generation because there is no easy way out of the cesspool of injustice and darkness aka planned doom.

Parents use to do whatever it took to make sure their children and young people turn out to be good citizens who respect the Creator's original plan and live by the Laws of Creation to the fullest without any mental and spiritual problems because everyone was taught about and knew the rules of the game of life. All parents must remember being imperfect is one of the basic laws of real parenting and it does not disqualify them from following, serving and teaching their children about the Creator's original plan and the Laws of Creation. Parents must teach their children and young people they have to continue fighting in the battle of good over evil at all times.

They must remember the Creator's original plan and the Laws of Creation is the BOSS OF ALL BOSSES: not disrespect, violent behavior, dishonor, and disunity. They all lead to self destruction and death happening. Over time the basics of real parenting which is having respect, love, and good intentions for one another will be a historic gamble that will pay off in the future big time. Satan and his Angels of Destruction continue building and establishing their monopoly of hopelessness, greed, disrespect, dishonor and disunity while trying to get rid of all competition.

Satan and his monopoly continue to come up with for new blue prints for their success while having respect, love, and good intentions for one another just sits on the side acting incompetent and it's time to fix what has been broken for decades. Parents must realize returning to the basics of true parenting will be one of the gutsiest moves they have made I centuries and it would eclipse Satan's monopoly. Parents are supposed to be the custodians of the truth and Keeping It Real; and it's time for preserving and the basic laws of true parenting.

Some parents now take for granted saying they are no longer needed anymore. These parents with this mindset now need a psychologist bench for a mental evaluation to see why they think having respect love, and good intentions for one another are not needed anymore in young people and children's lives. They need to read the newspaper, listen to the radio, or watch TV and they will see and get all the reasons why it's necessary for the return of having respect, love, and good intentions for one another as an everyday activity moving deeper into the century of the unknown.

Far too many young people and children have died and gotten locked away in the pit of doom, injustice and mental and spiritual misery for life. Parents must always remember that the basics of parenting which is teaching respect, love, and good intentions for one another use to be the engine of society. Children and young people are supposed to be the engineers who have the ultimate authority to keep this engine running. They must always try to figure out new ways to keep this engine running in the future. They can't afford to let this engine die; if it dies it will spell doom for society.

In the 21st century it seems like a lot of parents now have amnesia and have just given up on the basics of parenting.

It's time for them to get back to reality and become real parents.

GET BACK TO THE BASICS!

FOR PARENTS ONLY V
Starvation Coming
By
Mr. Dave R. Queeley

Parents must realize the harsh reality has set in, that they are children and young people are starving mentally and spiritually. They don't have the right tools and inspirations needed to move forward in the battle of good over evil. Starvation means to be deprived or caused to die from hunger. Young people and children are now hungry for the truth and no one in the Joe Bogus government or private sector is trying to feed them the knowledge so they can stay alive in the battle of good over evil.

It's time for society to feed young people and children the mental and spiritual food they need to become good citizens for the Creator, to be able to see the light of love, respect and good intentions for one another at the end of the tunnel. Parents have to teach the children and young people how to get off the treadmill of injustice, evil and darkness aka planned doom to that is now turning them into tyrants, who have no love and respect for the Creator's original plan and the Laws of Creation. They are now in need of mental and spiritual reform from the cradle to the grave.

They cannot live truly meaningful lives in a world full of spiritual ignorance and injustice, which now has no morals and standards to live by, only selfishness, greed and disunity. This leads to self-destruction and it's a serious problem to good winning the battle with evil. It's time to accelerate the downfall of the iron curtains of injustice, evil and darkness aka planned doom. The mental and spiritual situation in our communities and neighborhoods is now a catastrophe that is in need of a true solution.

Society must always remember. Prophecy is not being fulfilled; because they now have parents who do not have proper parenting skills, because it's now children giving birth to children. Their inability to teach their children about the Creator's original plan and the Laws of Creation is the main reason why so many of them are dying randomly, senselessly and unnecessarily from lack of knowledge and respect about self-love. They have forgotten about the number five law of Creation (COMMANDMENT), which is, "honor your father and mother that your days may be long."

How can they honor parents and the problem is children giving birth to children, and they lack maturity. Instead of being a parent, they try to be their children's friends. Now grand parents have to teach their grandchildren about the Creator's original plan and the Laws of Creation. The creators love is a feeling you can't fake; either you have it or you don't have it. The bottom line is the truth recognizes the truth. Hopelessness, disrespect, dishonor and disunity are now the evil Darth Vader, who continues to starve and torture young people and children mentally and spiritually to death in the 21st century.

The young people and children who are on how starving have forgotten that self-love and the realization that returning to having respect, love, respect and good intentions for one another will allow them to manifest in their most positive aspect in life, because negativity is inadequate and now worthless in the 21st century. If young people and children's mental and spiritual issues are not dealt with fixed fast it's going to lead to thousands of them starving to death in the future from not knowing the truth about the Creator's original plan and the Laws of Creation.

The enemies of the truth and doing what's right are always lurking and waiting to pounce on parents who have been slipping on their jobs and duty of being an inspiration to the mentally and spiritually dead children and young people, if parents start teaching their children and young people about the Creators original plan and the Laws of Creation. Maybe this will start healing the brokenness inside their hearts, souls and minds that make some of them commit a violent crime and assault. Parents need to start teaching their children and young people about the Creator's original plan and the Laws of Creation from an early age; it will help them stay free from the trap of greed is good and selfishness that leads them to the pit of injustice and misery.

The young people and children who are spiritually and mentally dead and starving for the truth must never forget THE TRUTH IS NEVER TEMPORARY AND KNOWLEDGE IS POWER and IGNORANCE IS SELF-DESTRUCTION. And it's a nuisance! They have to realize that returning to having respect, love, and good intentions for one another will provide young people and children who are spiritually and mentally dead with the useful tools for helping them to make healthier and better choices in their lives. They must never forget a good education is key to being mentally and spiritually successful and the return to having respect, love and good intentions will translate to the success of the Creator's original plan and the Laws of Creation, taking back our communities and neighborhoods from injustice and darkness aka planned doom.

It's time to put an end to this evil charade that continues to send young people and children to an early spiritual and mental grave. Parents must teach their children and young people who are mentally and spiritually dead and starving for the truth about what is written in the Bible a.k.a. The Good Book at Ecclesiastes C.1 V.9, "there is nothing new under the sun." So it's time to wake up and join the team of good over evil at all times. Young people and children must always remember. They are messengers of the Creator and have to keep their dignity and morals even when their feelings and loyalty to the Creator's original plan and the Love of Creation start slipping backwards, while the magical and invisible hand of hopelessness, disrespect, dishonor and disunity continue to choke the life out of them until they roll over and beg for mercy.

Hopelessness, disrespect, dishonor and disunity and are not compatible with the Creator's original plan and the laws because they are weapons of mass destruction also known as injustice and darkness aka planned doom. Parents cannot continue to be praised for the bad job they have been doing about teaching and spreading the Creator's original plan and the Laws of Creation to their children and young people. Children are born in love, but some of them are raised in hate. Hate is a darkness that they can't seem to escape from. That's why so many of them are still walking around spiritually and mentally dead in a starving for the truth because they continue signing up for Satan and his angels of destruction workforce that is going bankrupt and will be destroyed, which is on the not-too-distant horizon.

They will face corporal punishment for the deliberate disobedience to the Creator's original plan and the Laws of Creation. Young people and children who are now starving for the truth are not given frequent compliments and encouragement to stand up, speak out and fight for what's right and letting good intentions be the guiding light. If children get Nickelodeon and Disney and young people get MTV and BET on the television, parents don't have to say or do anything, they'll stay right there for hours. This is one of the main reasons why so many of them are now spiritually and mentally dead and starving for the truth in the 21st century.

 Young people and children are struggling to stay alive mentally and spiritually more than their parents are willing to acknowledge. Some of them are now playing Russian roulette with their lives. They have no foundation connecting them to the Creator's original plan and the Laws of Creation. It's time for them to board the convoy for the long journey back to having respect, love, and good intentions for one another as their highest and top priority in life.

PARENTS it's time to reverse this modern-day trend of letting young people and children grow up spiritually and mentally dead and starving to death for the truth.

IT'S TIME TO START FEEDING THEM BEFORE IT'S TOO LATE!

FOR PARENTS ONLY VI
Please Stand Up For Real
By
Mr. Dave R. Queeley

Parents cannot continue sticking their heads in the sands of denial, injustice and darkness aka planned doom. In the 21st century, there is now a lack of parental supervision and no financial support from government afterschool programs and activities. Parents are now convinced that politicians, our high-ranking government officials and their team of goons, also known as cronies intend to enact only superficial, economical, educational and healthcare reforms and change, so it can keep its hold on the monopoly of hopelessness, disrespect, dishonor and disunity.

What has been happening lately doesn't qualify as reform and change, but as dishonor to the people's vote. The principles and values of mediocrity by our high-ranking government officials and politicians must be rejected and should not be tolerated anymore. In the 21st century, mediocrity in government cannot be justified or explained: hopelessness disrespect, dishonor and disunity breeds' mediocrity. Politicians and our high-ranking government officials have been engines of injustice and darkness aka planned doom for too many years, they are not willing to step out of Satan and his angels of destruction shadow and start leading the people back to having respect, love, and good intentions for one another and to find true solutions to all the problems they face; that rising gas and food prices, failing public education and healthcare systems, and the high unemployment rate causes on a daily basis.

Parents are not proud of their government because there are no real community centers or afterschool programs for the children and young people to attend and enjoy themselves as children and young people without stress and fear of being hurt and killed. These programs will be one of the first steps that will help to keep them out of trouble and out of the pit of doom and injustice (jail or prison). Parents must always remember there are more Mahogany young males in prison or jail doing hard and long time, like 20 years or more, than there are in college seeking a degree. Parents must remember the consequences of physical slavery are social injustice and economic exploitation by Satan and his angels of destruction.

Satan continues renting his allies like politician, high-ranking government officials, police officers and religious leaders who continue to go to the highest bidder as long as there's money to be made in the backroom deals. These people in charge don't care what happens to the future generations. The public school system is crumbling with school closings, which seems like every summer. A good education doesn't lead to a life of crime and violence.

The BOC continues to build jails and prisons to lockup the perpetrators of these crimes who are getting younger and younger every day. Parents must never forget the reason they built prisons and jails and not schools; the pit of doom and injustice are now big business sold on the stock market, so someone is making money. Building schools will not make money, but will cost money. These people in charge are now drunk with power, full of disunity and their words empty of substance and truth. Now some parents feel used, because they voted for politicians and high-ranking government officials, who in return have given them and their children and young people one of the poorest education systems in the new world of injustice and darkness aka planned doom with the highest murder rate of any US territory. These people in charge have to invest in a quality public education system, and they must completely change the old one that continues to treat children like second class citizens and not like the future generation

Parents, politicians, police officers, religious leaders and our high-ranking government officials must always remember returning to having respect, love, and good intentions for one another will have all the components that is needed to be used to reshaping government, communities and neighborhoods from the paradise of negative (kill them all) back into the paradise of positive (love them all). They cannot continue to forget that in the 21st century, massive support from the younger generation will be necessary in making it possible.

The truth is, our communities and neighborhoods continue to take dips in the river or gutters of hopelessness, disrespect, dishonor and disunity. Some parents have dipped so deeply into these rivers or gutters of disrespect, dishonor and disunity, they can't stand up; so now they are drowning with no lifeguard insight to save them from self-destruction and death. If parents really care about their children's and young people's future success in life, now is the time for them to stand and speak out and fight for their children and young people's educational rights and future.

Since the circus is coming to town, also known as the election, now is the time to remind all politicians and our high-ranking government officials that the educational system in the world of injustice and darkness aka planned doom is now unraveling at the seams. Children and young people are the future generation of parents and grandparents, and they deserve better. The people in charge continue to play the game of Monopoly with our children and young people's future, while fake thuggery gun violence and crime continues to have them preoccupied with death and life in the pit of doom and injustice. These people in charge want parents to believe that children and young people's lives will not be affected by all those planned school closings and backroom deals they continue to make in the darkness of injustice and planned doom.

PARENTS PLEASE STAND UP, is the new message and wake-up call to let them know they should not let young people and children continue to embrace the negative stereotypes that are played out on television, and do things they know will make them appear to be foolish when they are not. In the 21st century, young people and children must be positive people in our communities and neighborhoods. They must return to having respect, love and good intentions for one another and do unto others as they would have done unto them, because it's all part of being a positive person, who has respect for the Creator's original plan and the Laws of Creation. If parents want change and reform, it's time they set better examples for young people and children to follow.

Parents are by no means the only culprit, politicians and high-ranking government officials, police officers and religious leaders also have to do their part in setting better examples too. Lately, their examples are incomplete and unsafe for young people and children who are mentally and spiritually dead to follow into this 21st century. These people have to provide a psychosocial environment, which will be conducive towards the growth in the Creator's original plan and the Laws of Creation to young people and children and to provide the protection they deserve from hopelessness, disrespect, dishonor and disunity. They are now ticking time bombs, getting ready to go off soon.

Hopelessness, disrespect, dishonor and disunity have become so much a part of young people and children's lives that their presence is felt even when they're not around. They all were once denounced in the past as threats to young people and children survival in the future. They now have lowered their intelligence and love about the Creator's original plan and The Laws of Creation. It also encourages them to skim the surface of knowledge and truth rather than dive headfirst into its depths, to see how deep it is.

The distraction that hopelessness, disrespect, dishonor and disunity causes are the beginning of self-destruction, and it's not a new phenomenon. They are now the new Phantom of the Opera. It shows that real parenting has gone to the dogs or pieces and it's now a lost art form in the 21st century. Unconsciously and consciously, parents are not speaking out, standing up and fighting for their children and young people's right to be educated properly about the Creator's original plan and the Laws of Creation parents must remember the original plan is GOOD WILL CONQUER EVIL AND LOVE WILL TRIUMPH OVER HATE. They have forgotten that some things in life are not worth the high price they have to pay like hopelessness, disrespect, dishonor and disunity, which leads to death or a very long time in the pit of doom and injustice (jail or prison) that leaves them spiritually and mentally bankrupt.

Parents are now out of sync when it comes to having respect, love, and good intentions for one another in their lives. In the 21st century, parents have to do whatever it takes to make sure the educational, economical, mental and spiritual future of their children and young people are secure for the next 500 years; like our ancestors did for us back in the good old days of good over evil at all times..

PARENTS PLEASE STAND UP!

The time has come to make something happen now and to never be scared, but to be prepared TO GIVE A HOOT and tell young people and children the truth about negative influences: because life is too short!

FOR PARENTS ONLY
DE END

Written by
Mr. Dave R. Queeley
10-30-2011

Made in the USA
Columbia, SC
29 October 2024

44929482R00041